VOLLEYBALL

FOR FUN!

By Darcy Lockman

Content Adviser: John Kessel, USA Volleyball, Colorado Springs, Colorado
Reading Adviser: Frances J. Bonacci, Ed.D., Reading Specialist, Cambridge, Massachusetts

COMPASS POINT BOOKS

MINNEAPOLIS, MINNESOTA

Compass Point Books
3109 West 50th Street, #115
Minneapolis, MN 55410

Visit Compass Point Books on the Internet at www.compasspointbooks.com
or e-mail your request to custserv@compasspointbooks.com

Photographs ©: Rubberball Productions, front cover (left), 12–13 (right), 23; Comstock Klips front cover (right), 12 (left), 42 (right); Corel front cover (background), 34-35, 36-37, 44, 45 (bottom), 47; Photodisc, 4-5, 42–43 (center), 43 (top), 45 (bottom); Millereau/DPPI-SIPA/Icon SMI, 7; AP/Wide World Photos, 8-9, 11, 18-19, 21, 24-25, 39, 40-41; Ingram Publishing, 13 (left), 45 (top); Istockphoto, 13 (right), 42 (left), 45 (top); Sergio Moraes/Reuters/Corbis, 15; Corbis/Roy Morsch, 16-17; Royalty Free/Corbis, 27; Alan Look/Icon SMI, 28-29; Stan Liu/Icon SMI, 30-31; Holly Stein/Icon SMI, 33; Glyn Kirk/Action Plus/Icon SMI, 38

Editors: Deb Berry and Aubrey Whitten/Bill SMITH STUDIO; and Shelly Lyons
Designer/Page Production: Geron Hoy, Kavita Ramchandran, Sinae Sohn, Marina Terletsky, and Brock Waldron/Bill SMITH STUDIO
Photo Researcher: Jacqueline Lissy Brustein, Scott Rosen, and Allison Smith/Bill SMITH STUDIO
Art Director: Jaime Martens
Creative Director: Keith Griffin
Editorial Director: Carol Jones
Managing Editor: Catherine Neitge

Library of Congress Cataloging-in-Publication Data
Lockman, Darcy, 1972-
 Volleyball for fun! / by Darcy Lockman.
    p. cm.—(Sports for fun!)
 Includes bibliographical references and index.
 ISBN 0-7565-1683-8 (hard cover)
 1. Volleyball—Juvenile literature. I. Title. II. Series.
 GV1015.34.L63 2006
 796.325—dc22   2005025220

Printed in the United States of America.

Table of Contents

Note: In this book, there are two kinds of vocabulary words. Volleyball Words to Know are words specific to volleyball and are defined on page 46. Other Words to Know are helpful words that aren't related only to volleyball and are defined on page 47.

The History of Volleyball

Volleyball is one of the most popular sports on the planet, second only to soccer in number of players worldwide. An estimated 800 million people participate in a volleyball game at least once each week. Are you one of them?

Volleyball was created by William G. Morgan in 1895. Morgan was an education director at a Massachusetts YMCA. He called it "mintonette" because it resembled badminton. Mintonette was played on a court divided by a 6 ½ foot (2 meter) net.

Originally, a team could have as few as one player on a side to an unlimited number of players. The players volleyed the ball back and forth across the net until one team missed and a point was scored. The first team to score 21 points was declared the winner.

People around the world helped create volleyball. YMCA missionaries and American military personnel taught the game internationally. Soon after its creation, volleyball was being played in Canada, Cuba, the Philippines, and China. World War I brought volleyball to Africa, as well as Western and Eastern Europe. Moves like spiking and blocking were created and perfected outside of the United States. Thanks to the hard work of players from many countries, including the United States, we have the Fédération Internationale de Volleyball (FIVB) to standardize play worldwide.

Where to Play Volleyball

Volleyball is played both indoors and outdoors, in gymnasiums, parks, and backyards, as well as on beaches. Though many people play for recreation on makeshift courts of any size, competitive games require that certain standards be met. The court must be 29½ feet by 59 feet (9 m by 18 m). It is divided into two squares by a center line. On indoor courts, an attack line is marked 9¾ feet (3 m) behind the center line on both sides. On sand volleyball courts, the attack lines are not visible. The sidelines mark the boundary of the sides of the court. The end lines or service lines mark the back of the court. The service area is behind the end line.

The net hangs directly above the center line. Its height can vary depending on the age of the players. Generally, though, the net is 7 feet 4⅛ inches (2.2 m) high for women and 7 feet 11⅝ inches (2.4 m) high for men. The poles that support the net should be 3 feet (.9 m) out on either side of the sideline. The ceiling should be at least 23 feet (7 m) high.

The Birth of Volleyball

Volleyball was created in the wake of excitement about the new game of basketball. William Morgan wanted to design an equally exhilarating but less strenuous game that could be played by middle-aged men.

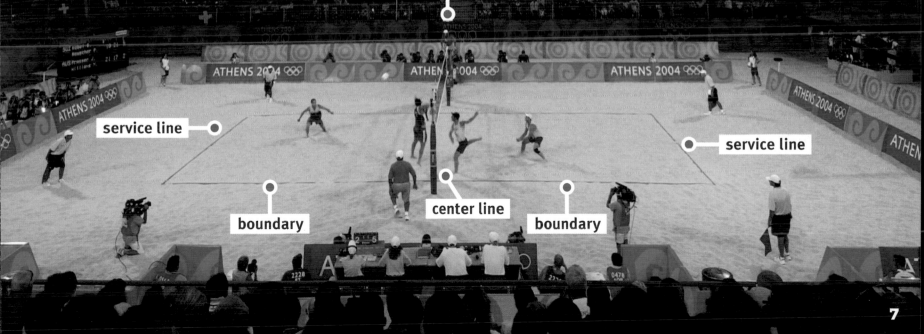

net

service line

service line

boundary

center line

boundary

The Roster

Volleyball is a team sport. Each team consists of six players, and the teams are divided on the court by a net. Three players stand near the net and three near the back line.

To begin, a player called a server attempts to hit the ball from anywhere behind the end line over the net. The other team must return the ball in no more than three hits without letting the ball touch the floor. The teams volley the ball back and forth until one team allows the ball to hit the ground. If it is the receiving team that allows the ball to hit the ground, the serving team serves again. If it is the serving team that allows this, the receiving team becomes the serving team. This is called a side-out.

Volleyball players do not stand in the same spot for the entire game. Players move clockwise one position every time their team gets the side-out. In volleyball, this is called rotating.

What's in a Name?

William Morgan originally used a tennis net for his game, raising it 6½ feet (2 m) off the ground. Mintonette got its own net after it became "volleyball" in 1895 when a spectator at a demonstration game commented that the game involved a lot of volleying.

Ready, Set, Score!

The object of the game in volleyball is to send the ball regularly over the net to the opposing team in an effort to ground the ball on their side of the court. While doing this, players must also keep the ball from touching down on their own side.

In returning the ball to the opponents, a team is allowed to hit the ball three times. A player may not hit a ball more than once in a single turn. In returning the ball, players must also be careful not to hit the ball outside the lines of the court.

A point is scored each time the volley is disrupted. The game continues until one team reaches a set number of points, usually 15 or 25.

Going for the Win

In volleyball, matches are comprised of three or five games. The team that wins two of three, or three of five games wins the match.

Gearing Up for the Game

Whether you're playing indoor or outdoor volleyball, on a court or in the sand, two things you will always need are a volleyball and a net. If you're playing beach volleyball, a healthy dose of sunshine doesn't hurt either!

A volleyball is about the same size as a soccer ball, but it is softer and lighter. Made of either leather or synthetic leather, it is inflated with air and weighs between 9 and 10 ounces (about 270 grams). Its circumference is approximately 26 inches (66 centimeters).

Volleyball players usually wear uniforms consisting of shorts and short-sleeved jerseys. Each player has a different number.

A good pair of volleyball shoes will allow for a good grip on the court and help defend against ankle sprains and dangerous falls.

To protect their knees and elbows, volleyball players often wear knee and elbow pads. Some also wear palm guards to protect their hands and wrists from the impact of the ball, as well as from falls.

Sizing Up Nets

A standard volleyball net is 32½ feet (10 m) long and 3¼ feet (1 m) wide. They are made of nylon and mesh and are bound on the edges and sides.

Putting the Ball in Play

To begin play in volleyball, a player on the serving team serves by throwing the ball up into the air and hitting it over the net into the opposing team's court. The server is positioned in the back row on the right side and stands behind the end line. The server cannot step back into the court until he or she has touched the ball. The server cannot take more than eight seconds to serve. If the server throws the ball into the air and misses, he or she will sometimes be allowed to re-toss. If the ball is served under the net, into the net, or out of bounds, it is called a service fault, and the serve goes to the other team.

A server can serve underhand or overhand. For an underhand serve, the ball is held at waist level. The player leans forward while swinging one arm forward to contact the ball. The hand holding the ball is removed just before contact with the ball, and the ball is hit with either the fist or the heel of the hand. For an overhand serve, the player tosses the ball above his or her head about 18 inches (46 cm). With elbow and hand at shoulder height, the player shifts his or her weight forward and hits the ball with the fist or heel of the hand.

Serving with Style

Different types of serves include a sky ball serve, a spin serve, a jump serve, and a roundhouse serve, just to name four. Like clothing, serves come in and out of fashion.

Get on the Ball!

The team with possession of the ball is on offense. It is the offensive team's job to ground the ball on the side of the opposing team, thereby scoring a point and either winning or maintaining the serve.

The team on offense must use no more than three hits to move the ball to the other team's court. These three hits occur in a somewhat predictable order, from a pass to a set to a spike. The pass moves the ball along to the player designated as a setter. The setter sets the ball with an overhand pass using the fingertips. He or she then puts the ball into position in the air for the player he or she chooses to be the attacker. The attacker then spikes the ball, or jumps up to hit it so that it moves forcefully and quickly over the net to the ground of the opposing team's court.

Passing the Ball

There are two types of passes: the overhead pass and the bump. A bump is performed by extending the arms and joining the hands at waist height before hitting the ball with the forearms. An overhead pass is performed with the fingertips above the head. After the ball is passed to the setter, the setter sets the ball to the attacker, who then spikes or hits it over the net.

Stopping Points

The team on defense has to stop the opposing team's attacker from grounding the ball on their side of the court. They do this by blocking the attacked ball. To perform a block, a player standing at the net jumps up and reaches above it to try to stop the ball before it even makes it over the net. Sometimes the blocker keeps the ball from coming over the net, but sometimes this is not possible.

If the ball gets past the blocker, another defensive player will attempt to stop the ball with a dig. A dig is an underarm pass of a hard-driven ball. A digger extends his or her arms at the waist and joins the hands in order to hit the ball with the forearms. Because the ball is usually coming fast and hard, sometimes players must dive toward the floor to perform a dig. If the dig is successful, the defensive team is then on offense and must begin the task of passing, setting, and spiking.

Slam Those Points!

There are two types of scoring common in volleyball: side-out scoring and rally-point scoring. In all but a few nations, rally-point scoring is always used.

In side-out scoring, points can only be scored by the team that has the service. If the serving team makes an error or the ball is grounded on their side of the court, no point is scored, but their term of service ends. This means the other team begins to serve and has the opportunity to score points. When side-out scoring is used, games are usually played up to 15 points.

In rally-point scoring, points are either scored by the team that successfully grounds the ball on the other team's side or by the team that doesn't make an error. The team who wins the point is awarded the next serve. If the team that wins the point was not the last team to serve, the players rotate clockwise one position. In rally-point scoring, the first team to score 25 points wins the game. In college, however, the first team to score 30 points wins.

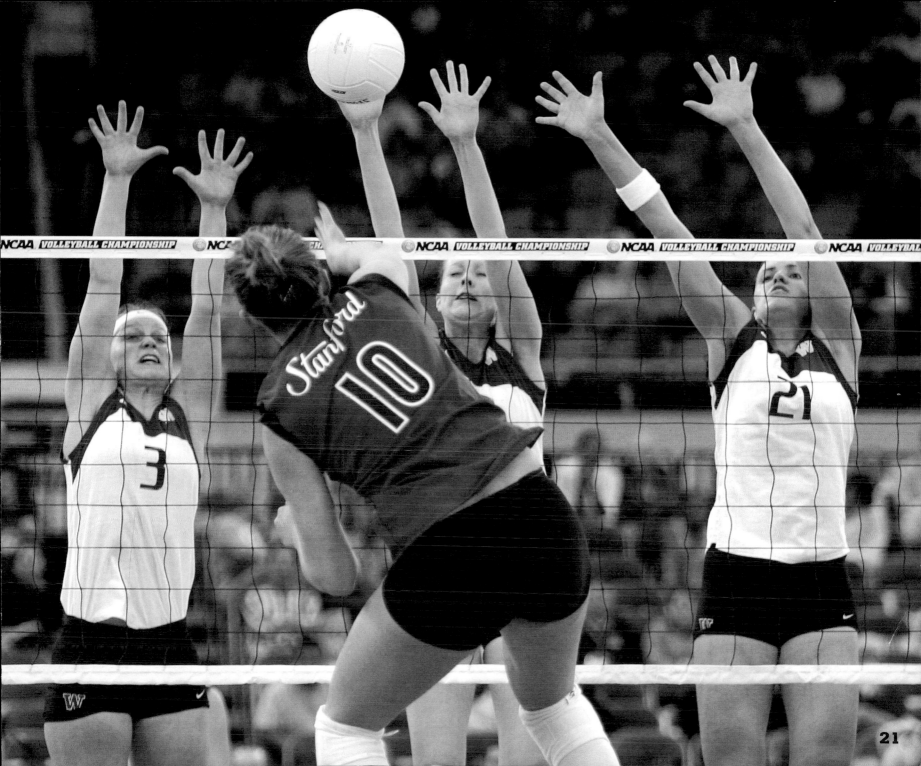

Playing the Ball

The set is generally the second move made by an offensive team. The setter is very important, because he or she makes decisions about the team's offensive plays. The setter's job is to position the ball so that it can be driven hard and fast into the other team's court. In positioning the ball in this way, the setter is responsible for deciding which teammate will spike the ball.

As in passing, there are two kinds of sets: the overhand and the bump. The overhand set is performed with the fingertips, holding the arms over the head. The bump is performed below the waist with the forearms. Sometimes the setter hits the ball over the net rather than set it up for an attacker. This move is called a dump.

The spike is usually the offensive team's third and final contact with the ball before they switch to defense. The attacker tries to spike, or hit the ball hard enough that the opposing team cannot return it. To do this, the attacker approaches the ball with several steps, jumps up, and throws his or her weight forward to hit the ball forcefully over the net. Modern volleyball includes many types of attacks other than spikes. These include backcourt attacks, cross-court shots, tips, and off-speed hits, just to name a few.

TV Nation!

Side-out scoring was the only type of scoring used until recently. In 2000, the rule was changed to rally-point scoring in order to make the length of the match more predictable. This made volleyball easier to televise and keeps tournaments and leagues from running into overtime.

Preventing the Point

After the team on offense has attacked the ball, it's the defensive team's goal to stop it from hitting the ground on their side of the court. They try two different moves, the block and the dig.

A block can be either offensive or defensive. The block is usually attempted when the other team has spiked the ball. Blocks are performed by jumping in the air while lifting the arms over the net, shortly before or as the ball is being hit. An offensive block is an attempt to score on the block by putting the ball right back in the attacking team's court. A defensive block is not an attempt to return the ball, but rather slows down the spike so that the blocker's teammates can dig.

Digging is the attempt to stop the ball from touching the ground after a spike or other attack. Digging is performed either overhand or with a bump.

Hit the Floor!

Sometimes digging players must drop to the floor in order to bump. When a player just makes it under a ball that is almost touching the floor, it is called a pancake because the player and his or her hands are flat against the floor.

Oops! Can't Do That!

There are many ways to make errors in volleyball. A server can make a service error when the ball does not land within the opposing team's court, or the player commits a foot fault. This happens when his or her foot touches the court inside the end line before touching the ball.

An attacker can make an attack error by stepping over the court's center line, landing the ball out of bounds, or hitting the ball into the net on an attack. A blocking player can make a blocking error by stepping over the court's center line, blocking from the back row, or reaching over the net.

Any player can commit a ball handling error when the ball is handled improperly. A reception error occurs when a player moves to receive a ball, but either misses it or fails to keep it in play. Finally, there are additional things that players are not allowed to do, like touching the net, serving out of turn, and taking more than eight seconds to serve the ball.

Most Common Goofs

The most common ball handling errors include double hits, when one player hits the ball two times or more in a single turn; throws, when a player grabs and throws the ball; and lifts, when a player holds a ball during contact.

The Role of the Referee

The person who makes decisions about play during a volleyball game is the referee. The referee is responsible for making sure that players and coaches follow the rules. Volleyball games usually have two referees, one to monitor each side of the court. He or she calls points and errors, makes sure the players are in position during the serve, and decides when balls are in and out of bounds.

Referees also make sure that players and coaches follow proper volleyball etiquette. The rules of etiquette differ in different places, but players and coaches are expected to demonstrate good sportsmanship. Additionally, players and coaches should not question or try to influence the referee's decision about a play.

Seeing Red

If a referee doesn't like a player or coach's behavior, he or she might flash a yellow card as a warning. A second flash of the yellow card can result in a player or coach being disqualified from a match. A red card is a more severe penalty given by the official to a player or coach. A red card gives a point to the non-offending team.

Decisions, Decisions

A good coach motivates all the players to put forth their best effort. To do this, volleyball coaches work closely with their teams during both practices and matches. During practice, it is common for coaches to perform gamelike drills with their teams. Drills are practice moves that aim to develop a variety of volleyball skills like ball control and passing.

During games, coaches make important decisions about a team's play. These decisions include when to call time-out, and when to take a player off the court and replace him or her with another player. Teams are generally allowed either a one minute time-out or two 30-second time-outs per game. Coaches use the time to discuss strategy with the players. Coaches are also allowed to make substitutions during time-outs, and may do so if a player is injured or playing poorly.

Here's to You, Coach!

Coaches' decisions are often based on years of experience. Many coaches were once volleyball players themselves and have taken their love for playing the game and turned it into a love for teaching the game.

A New Deal

The game of volleyball changed in 1998 when a new position was added to the game. The libero can replace any other player at any point during a game. The libero specializes in defensive skills and is not allowed to block or attack. The libero is usually not allowed to serve. So the libero can be distinguished, he or she wears a different colored jersey from the other players.

Also in 1998, the rules changed to allow any part of the body to touch the ball. Before this change, any time the ball touched the body below the waist, a foul was called.

In 2000 even more rule changes were put into play. The net serve was introduced. It is a serve that touches the net and then continues into the opponent's court. The net serve is an acceptable serve in some volleyball leagues, but in others it is not.

Finally, the same year saw the expansion of the service area to any spot behind the end line and within the sidelines. Even after passing its 100th birthday, the sport of volleyball is continuing to evolve!

Ways to Play It

Traditional volleyball has inspired creative sports enthusiasts to try volleyball with a twist. One of these twists is blind volleyball. The traditional volleyball net is replaced with a thick tarp. Because the players cannot see the opposing team, they have a more difficult time predicting how and when the ball will return to them. Because of this, blocks, spikes, and overhand serves are prohibited.

Sitting volleyball was introduced in 1956 in Holland to allow disabled players to participate in the sport. Because the game is played while seated on the floor, the court is smaller and the net is lower.

Nine-man volleyball is another version of the game. It utilizes nine players and a slightly larger court. Nine-man volleyball originated in Asia, and today is most popular in Chinese-American communities in large cities in the United States.

Guys and Gals

Co-ed volleyball features men and women playing on the same team. Male and female players must alternate in the service order. For every three offensive hits made by a team, at least one must be carried out by a woman.

Playing in the Sand

The most popular and well-known variation of volleyball is beach volleyball. Though originally a recreational sport created in the 1920s by bored California sunbathers, beach volleyball today is a competitive sport that is played by men and women in the Olympics. Beach volleyball is played on sand courts that are 52 feet by 26 feet (16 m by 8 m). However, the biggest difference between traditional volleyball and beach volleyball is the number of players per team. In beach volleyball, two players compete against two other players to win games and matches. Beach volleyball can also be played for fun with multiple players.

A newer version of beach volleyball is indoor sand volleyball. Played on a basketball court covered with a tarp and a foot (30 cm) of soft sand, indoor volleyball teams have from two to six players.

Fun in the Sun and Sand

Sand provides more cushioning than a hard floor, so volleyball played on sand is less likely to result in injury than traditional volleyball. Because of this, many leagues are making the switch from hard court to indoor sand volleyball.

The Famous Faces of Volleyball

CHARLES "KARCH" KIRALY
Born in Jackson, Michigan, in November 1960, three-time Olympic gold medalist Charles Kiraly was named the Greatest Volleyball Player of the 20th Century by the International Federation of Volleyball. Kiraly's gold medals are not only for indoor, but also for beach volleyball. He began playing when he was only 6 years old, encouraged by his father, a former Hungarian Junior National team player. Kiraly was a star player in high school and college. By 1984 he was playing in the Olympics in Los Angeles, where he was the youngest player on the gold-medal winning U.S. team. In 1995, the FIVB named him the best volleyball player in the 21st century and in 2001 he was named to the Volleyball Hall of Fame.

DANIELLE SCOTT

Danielle Scott was born in October 1972 in Baton Rouge, Louisiana. The 6 foot 2 inch (185 cm) two-time Olympian is considered by many to be one of the best blockers in the world. Her career in sports has been long and varied. Though volleyball has always been her best event, she has also been a basketball star, even earning a try-out with the U.S. women's pro league, the Women's National Basketball Association (WNBA). Aside from her Olympic volleyball appearances in 1996, 2000, and 2004, Scott has also participated in two Pan American Games, one world championship, and two World University Games. Scott recently returned to the U.S. National Team after an impressive turn playing professional volleyball in Brazil, where she became known as the Shaquille O'Neal of volleyball.

Going for the Gold

Spectators first watched volleyball at the Olympics in 1924 not as a competitive event, but as part of a demonstration of American sports. It was not until 1964 in Tokyo that volleyball was first played for an Olympic medal. Ten men's teams and six women's teams competed. That year, the gold went to the former Soviet Union men's team and Japan women's team.

In 1984 the United States won its first volleyball medals: the gold for the men and the silver for the women. In 1996, volleyball attracted much attention when beach volleyball became an Olympic sport and the United States won gold and silver medals. The fast-paced, two-person games drew large crowds and transformed beach volleyball from a virtually unknown sport to one with its own superstars and devoted fans.

Getting Better All the Time

Participation among countries has increased enormously since volleyball was first introduced as an official Olympic sport. There are 12 spots available for both men's and women's Olympic indoor teams. Beach Olympic teams have 12 available spots for men and 12 for women. Teams qualify for the Olympics by winning various qualification tournaments, and competition is often intense.

What Happened When?

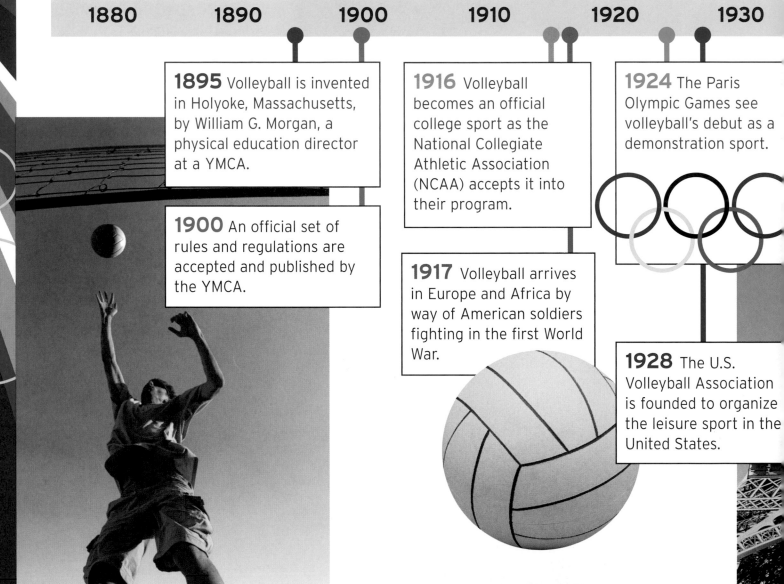

1880	1890	1900	1910	1920	1930

1895 Volleyball is invented in Holyoke, Massachusetts, by William G. Morgan, a physical education director at a YMCA.

1900 An official set of rules and regulations are accepted and published by the YMCA.

1916 Volleyball becomes an official college sport as the National Collegiate Athletic Association (NCAA) accepts it into their program.

1917 Volleyball arrives in Europe and Africa by way of American soldiers fighting in the first World War.

1924 The Paris Olympic Games see volleyball's debut as a demonstration sport.

1928 The U.S. Volleyball Association is founded to organize the leisure sport in the United States.

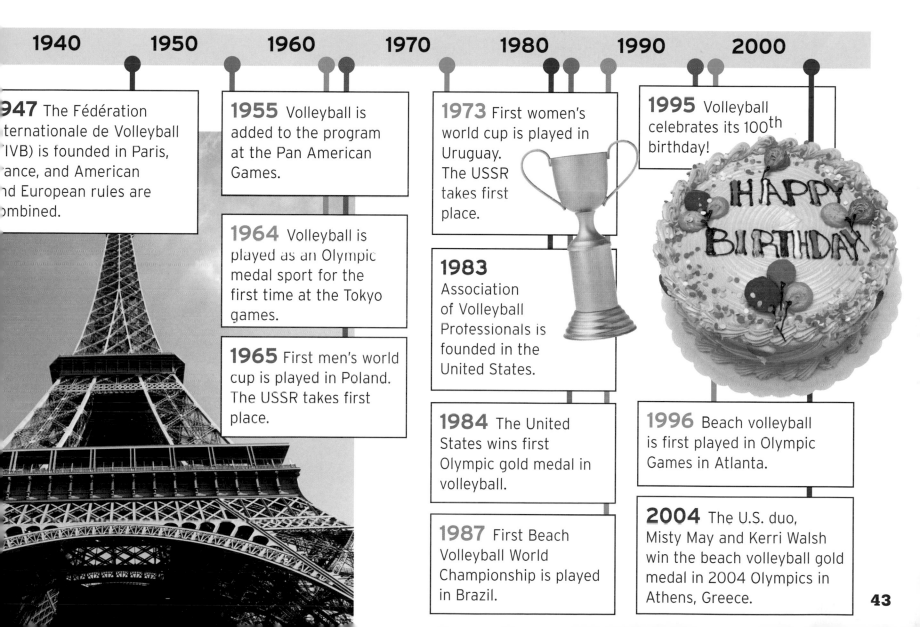

1940   **1950**   **1960**   **1970**   **1980**   **1990**   **2000**

947 The Fédération
ternationale de Volleyball
IVB) is founded in Paris,
rance, and American
nd European rules are
ombined.

1955 Volleyball is
added to the program
at the Pan American
Games.

1964 Volleyball is
played as an Olympic
medal sport for the
first time at the Tokyo
games.

1965 First men's world
cup is played in Poland.
The USSR takes first
place.

1973 First women's
world cup is played in
Uruguay.
The USSR
takes first
place.

1983
Association
of Volleyball
Professionals is
founded in the
United States.

1984 The United
States wins first
Olympic gold medal in
volleyball.

1987 First Beach
Volleyball World
Championship is played
in Brazil.

1995 Volleyball
celebrates its 100th
birthday!

1996 Beach volleyball
is first played in Olympic
Games in Atlanta.

2004 The U.S. duo,
Misty May and Kerri Walsh
win the beach volleyball gold
medal in 2004 Olympics in
Athens, Greece.

Fun Volleyball Facts

Volleyball legends Karch Kiraly, Sinjin Smith, and Jeff Nygaard all went to UCLA university.

In the beginning, teams were allowed to have as many players as would fit on the court!

Canada was the first country outside of the United States to play volleyball.

During the Great Depression in the 1930s, beach volleyball offered those who had suffered financial loss a great escape from their troubles.

The Cuban women's volleyball team has been the strongest team to date. They have won three consecutive Olympic gold medals, making them unbeatable for almost two decades.

Several countries experimented with time-limited volleyball games that were played for a certain number of minutes rather than up to a set number of points. Time-limited volleyball, though, never really caught on.

Spiking was developed in the Philippines and became known as "the Filipino bomb."

Volleyball was recommended by chiefs of staff for training troops during World War II. The military believed it would keep troops in shape and teach them to work together as a group.

Volleyball Words to Know

attack line: the lines parallel to the center line that separate the frontcourt from the backcourt; backcourt players must attack the ball from behind this line

backcourt attack: attack carried out by a player standing in the back row

bump: a move performed by an offensive player intended to move the ball toward the player designated as a setter

center line: the line under the net that separates the two sides of the court

cross-court shot: an attack that moves diagonally across the court

dig: this defensive move, performed to stop an attacked ball, is an underarm pass with the forearms of a hard-hit ball

end line: the line marking the very back of the court on both sides

ground: the action in volleyball of causing the ball to hit the floor on the other team's court

jump serve: overhead serve where the ball is tossed high and hit by jumping high above the endline with a strong downward movement of the arm

off-speed hit: an attack in which the player hits the ball gently in order to slow it down and confuse the opponent

overhead serve: the player throws the ball up in the air and hits it when it's above shoulder height

roundhouse serve: the player stands with one shoulder to the net, throws the ball high, and hits it with a speedy, circular movement of the arm

service area: the area on the court from which it is legal to serve

service line: the endline; servers must serve from inside these lines

set: an overhead pass using the finger tips intended to position the ball for a teammate to spike

side-out: the receiving team wins the rally against the serving team; the receiving team then becomes the serving team

sky ball serve: type of underhand serve where the ball is hit so high it comes down almost in a straight line

spike: to jump, raise one arm above the head, and hit the ball so it will move forcefully and quickly over the net to the ground of the opponent's court

spin serve: overhead serve where the player snaps his or her wrist to give the ball top-spin

term of service: any consecutive period during which one team has the serve

tip: an attack in which an offensive player hits the ball lightly to an area of the opponent's court not being covered by the defense

underhand serve: the player strikes the ball from below or at waist level. This serve is considered the easiest to return

GLOSSARY
Other Words to Know

disrupt: to interrupt the course of a process or activity

enthusiast: someone who is very interested or involved in something, particularly a hobby

etiquette: the rules and conventions governing correct or polite behavior

makeshift: a temporary and usually inferior substitute

motivate: to give somebody a reason or incentive to do something

obscure: not important or well-known

standardize: make the same

strategy: a carefully devised plan of action to achieve a goal

strenuous: physically challenging

tarp: a heavy sheet of waterproof material

transform: change completely for the better.

Where To Learn More

AT THE LIBRARY

Dearing, Joel. *Volleyball Fundamentals*. Champagne, IL.: Human Kinetics Publishers, 2003.

Kiraly, Karch. *Karch Kiraly's Championship Volleyball*. New York: Fireside Books, 1996.

ON THE ROAD

Volleyball Hall of Fame
444 Dwight St.
Holyoke, MA 01040
413/536-0926

ON THE WEB

For more information on this topic, use FactHound.

1. Go to *www.facthound.com*
2. Type in this book ID: 0756516838
3. Click on the *Fetch It* button.

FactHound will find the best Web sites for you.

INDEX

ABOUT THE AUTHOR

Darcy Lockman is a writer and editor. Her work has appeared in the *New York Times*, *Rolling Stone* and *Seventeen*, among others. The author of several other nonfiction books for children, she lives in Brooklyn, New York, where she is currently at work on a series of mystery novels.